FRANKLIN D. ROOSEVELT

Adrian Gilbert

RAINTREE
STECK-VAUGHN
PUBLISHERS

A Harcourt Company

Austin   New York
www.raintreesteckvaughn.com

First published 2003 by Raintree Steck-Vaughn Publishers, an imprint of Steck-Vaughn Company.

©2002 Franklin Watts

Library of Contress Cataloging-in-Publication Data

ISBN 0-7398-5260-4

Printed in Hong Kong/China. Bound in the United States.

1 2 3 4 5 6 7 8 9 0 LB 05 04 03 02

Designer Michele Ashby
Editor Constance Novis
Raintree Editors Sean Dolan, Walter Kossman
Art Director Jonathan Hair
Editor-in-Chief John C. Miles

Picture credits
Front cover and Back cover:
©Hulton/Archive
(Background); Peter Newark's
American Pictures (main)
AKG London pp.21, 26–27, 45, 49, 54, 60–61, 63, 71, 72-73, 74–75, 82-83, 96
Courtesy of the Franklin D. Roosevelt Library Digital Archives pp. 15, 31, 100–101
Peter Newark's American Pictures pp. 2, 3, 5, 11, 12–13, 22, 25, 32, 35, 46, 47, 67, 68, 79, 80, 84, 88–89, 92-93, 95, 99
Popperfoto pp. 9, 17, 19, 29, 30, 38–39, 40–41, 42–43, 50, 53, 56-57, 59, 64, 70, 86–87, 105
Topham Picturepoint pp. 6–7, 37, 103

F. D. Roosevelt
1882–1945

Contents

Introduction

Franklin D. Roosevelt was an extraordinary person, considered by many to be the greatest American president of the 20th century. The British prime minister Winston Churchill, who worked closely with Roosevelt during World War II, said his life "must be regarded as one of the commanding events in human destiny."

By nature, Roosevelt—affectionately known as "FDR"—was kindhearted and cheerful. These characteristics were evident in his style of presidency. One of his great strengths was being able to communicate with people from all walks of life. He came from a wealthy, almost aristocratic background, and he was never in awe of rich industrialists, politicians, or other world leaders. At the same time, however, he was always at ease with the ordinary man and woman on the street. People sensed that he was able to empathize with their problems.

Roosevelt certainly aroused strong emotions. He was both loved and hated. For the poor and needy who had been hit hardest by the Great Depression, he became something of a savior figure. One Texas furniture worker wrote to him at the White House, "You are the one and only President that ever helped a Working Class of People." On hearing of Roosevelt's death, a young soldier observed, "I felt as if I knew him. I felt as if he knew me—and I felt as if he liked me."

These feelings of warmth held by millions of Americans were not universal. Many (usually better-off) people despised Roosevelt. Some even refused to use his name, calling him "that man in the White House"! He was accused of being a "traitor to his class" and a power-mad politician who would do anything to stay in office. Whatever people thought of him on a personal level, however, there could be no doubt about Roosevelt's importance as a statesman, and the lasting influence he had over the 20th century.

▶ *Franklin Roosevelt is the only man to be elected to four terms as president of the United States.*

A Privileged Upbringing

Franklin Delano Roosevelt was born on January 30, 1882. His parents were wealthy and came from the privileged classes who enjoyed power and influence throughout the United States.

Franklin's father, James Roosevelt, could trace his ancestry back to the original Dutch settlers who had left Holland for America in the 1640s. His mother, Sara Delano, was descended from the Puritans who landed at Plymouth, Massachusetts, in 1621.

Although James Roosevelt had a number of business interests, he was rich enough to be able to spend most of his time at his estate, called Springwood, near the village of Hyde Park in New York State. There he lived the life of a country gentleman, looking after the property and breeding horses.

James was a widower. At the late age of 52 he married his new wife, Sara, a woman of only 26. Two years after the wedding Franklin was born. Despite his fairly advanced years, James taught Franklin how to swim, skate, ride a horse, and sail a boat. Although father and son had a close relationship, Franklin's mother was the dominant force: she organized every aspect of his life, and even when he was an adult she continued to fuss over him.

◀ *The Roosevelt family home at Hyde Park, in New York State.*

Franklin led a rather isolated existence. He was an only child and was not allowed to play with the local children since they were considered "unsuitable" for a boy of his class. As a result, he spent most of his time alone or with adults.

Franklin did not go to school in his early years but was educated at home by governesses and then by a private tutor. He was taught all the usual subjects, which at that time included French, Latin, history, geography, science, and math.

A Happy Childhood

Although he might have seemed lonely, Franklin had a happy childhood. He was allowed to roam through the estate and had many hobbies. He enjoyed horseback riding, photography, collecting bird eggs, and shooting—an activity that was common for boys at that time. Between the ages of 11 and 14, Franklin shot, stuffed, and mounted 300 different species of bird from his native Dutchess County, a collection still maintained at his old Springwood home. In quieter moments Franklin read books or built up his large stamp collection.

There were vacations in both America and Europe; by the age of 14 Franklin had already crossed the Atlantic eight times. Every year the family went to their summer home at Campobello, an island off the coast of New Brunswick, Canada. There he learned to sail, first on his father's yacht, *Half Moon*, and then on his own smaller sailboat, *New Moon*. Franklin became a good sailor, and his love of the sea and ships was to be another long-lasting interest.

Franklin lived a pampered life, where everything was provided for him, and yet he was not spoiled. His parents could be very strict, and he was taught to be polite and well-mannered at all times—and to work hard at his studies. His mother said, "His father and I always expected a great deal of Franklin. After all, he had many advantages that other boys did not." The young Roosevelt was generally happy; he liked to have fun, and looked forward to meeting people.

Most boys of his background went to boarding school at the age of 12, but his mother could not bear his leaving the family home. So it was only at the age of 14 that Franklin was sent to his first school, Groton.

▶ *An early picture of baby Franklin with his mother, Sara Roosevelt.*

Life at Groton

Located in the nearby state of Massachusetts, Groton was an exclusive institution, modeled after British public schools. It prepared boys for entry into America's top universities, such as the "Ivy League" colleges.

Groton's founder and headmaster, the Reverend Endicott Peabody, was a huge presence in the school and had a great influence on Franklin. Because his pupils came from wealthy backgrounds, Endicott believed that they should develop a sense of social responsibility for those less well off than they were. He also believed that Groton scholars should do something useful with their lives and devote themselves to the service of their country. In response, Franklin helped out at a summer camp run by the school for poor children from the cities of Boston and New York.

Arriving two years later than the other boys of his age, Franklin found life at Groton hard. The others were already settled in, but Franklin had to start from scratch to find friends and make a name for himself in a very ambitious school. Wanting to be accepted, Franklin tried to do well in sports, but at the age of 14 he was too thin to excel in the team games that really counted at Groton. In football he was picked only for the seventh team, and it was much the same story in baseball. But Franklin persevered, and he worked his way through the football system to make it to the second team. His determination to succeed showed strength of character, but his early years at Groton were not happy ones. As a father he later sent his own sons there—but at the age of 12, so that they could adapt to school life more easily.

In his academic work he did well but not brilliantly, and he was praised for his neatness and punctuality. At one point, Franklin was worried that he would become unpopular with the other boys because of his punctuality, and he deliberately got a bad mark for being late.

In 1897 the rising politician Theodore Roosevelt—a distant cousin of Franklin's —came to speak at Groton. It was a major occasion for the school, and for Franklin, who had come to see his relative as a role model.

▶ *Franklin's cousin Theodore Roosevelt. "Teddy" was an up-and-coming politician in 1897, when he came to speak to the boys at Groton School.*

The following year "Cousin Teddy" was elected governor of New York, and Franklin and his family attended the inauguration, which planted in Franklin's mind the idea that politics might work out to be a promising career for him.

A Rising Talent

As time went by, Franklin began to feel more at home at Groton. At the end of his four years he was made a dormitory prefect, had moved up through the football team system, and had become manager of the baseball team. His academic work was steadily improving, and he was considered one of the best debaters in the school. And, most importantly, Franklin had achieved his goal of finding a degree of popularity among the other boys. As time went on he would develop this skill and become the sort of person that people liked to be with—an invaluable tool for a successful politician. When he left Groton in 1900 to go to Harvard, Franklin had a newfound sense of self-confidence.

◀ *Groton school photograph. Franklin Roosevelt is in the front row, second from the left.*

Harvard and Marriage

Franklin Roosevelt enrolled at Harvard University in September 1900 to study history and government. As one of the premier universities in the country, Harvard attracted America's most talented and wealthy students.

Franklin established himself in a two-room apartment (which he shared with a Groton classmate) in one of the better areas of town, away from the dormitories at the university that the poorer students had to share. He also joined an exclusive dining club that had a special table for ex-Groton students. Franklin felt very much at home, telling his parents that the club was "great fun."

Like many other students at Harvard, Franklin did not take study that seriously. He did enough work to get by and devoted most of his spare time to other activities. He wrote home to his mother that he was engaged in "a little studying, a little riding, and a few party calls." Sports continued to be a major interest, and although he did not make any of the

Harvard

Harvard College was founded in 1636 and was named after John Harvard, its chief benefactor. Originally intended to educate Puritan ministers, it later expanded its curriculum to include a wider range of studies, and by the mid-19th century it had become one of the world's foremost universities.

Harvard was a male-only university until as late as 1969, but a women's college—Radcliffe—was founded in 1879 and coexisted alongside the main university.

university teams, he played football and joined a rowing club.

Life at Harvard revolved around the many college social clubs. Franklin was

▶ The Harvard class of 1904 at the beach. Franklin is the tall figure in the center of the back row.

Job No :CG 02-008
Job Title: 20th Century History Maker Roosevelt
Client : The Watt Group

Trim Size :W 187 mm X H 229 ···
Paper Stock : Matt Art

invited to join the Institute of 1770, a springboard for the more exclusive societies that would guarantee social success as a Harvard student. While he was made a member of the secret Delta Kappa Epsilon, Franklin was not invited to join Harvard's elite Porcellian Society. The pain he felt was worsened by the knowledge that his own father had been an honorary member. Franklin later told a friend that "this was the greatest disappointment of my life." The reasons for being snubbed by the Porcellian were never known, but for the first time Franklin knew the feeling of rejection.

Journalistic Ambitions

Franklin did find success in another area of student life—working on the daily college newspaper, the *Harvard Crimson*. Competition for this job was fierce, but Franklin got in. He was not a great reporter, although he did gain a scoop when he alone found out that Theodore Roosevelt (now vice president of the United States) was going to speak to the students at Harvard. But Franklin worked hard, and over the years he rose to become the paper's president and editor in chief.

While Franklin was at Harvard, his father died at the age of 72. He had suffered from heart problems for some time and while his death was not a surprise, it was still a shock for Franklin and his mother Sara. But more of a surprise was Sara's decision to leave the family home at Hyde Park and come to live in Boston to be closer to Franklin. With her husband gone, Sara devoted herself totally to Franklin's welfare, despite the fact that he was now a man in his own right. Franklin, for his part, did not seem to mind his mother's overly possessive attitude.

Meeting Eleanor

At Franklin's 21st birthday celebration in January 1903, a distant cousin named Eleanor Roosevelt was invited to the party at Hyde Park. Although the two had met before, it was only during the summer of 1903 that they began to see each other regularly, especially after Franklin invited Eleanor to Campobello Island.

▶ *Eleanor Roosevelt (right) pictured with Sara, Franklin's mother, at the time of her engagement.*

Eleanor was very different from Franklin. Whereas he was confident, friendly, and outgoing, she was shy and retiring—but they were attracted to each other. Both of Eleanor's parents had died when she was young (her alcoholic father was the younger brother of Theodore Roosevelt), and she had had an unhappy childhood until sent to boarding school in England when she was 15. Eleanor enjoyed being at school, but after three years she was called back home where, as a young lady, she made her formal debut in society and was required to attend balls and parties. Eleanor—a serious and rather plain girl—found the frivolous social scene "utter agony."

A Society Wedding

Franklin proposed to her on November 21, 1903, and Eleanor said yes. Franklin was overjoyed, but his mother was against the marriage. She thought they were too young (Franklin was 21, Eleanor only 19) and she was also concerned that she might lose influence over her son. But in the end she approved the match, although the couple were made to keep their engagement a secret for a year. They were married on March 17, 1905, in New York. The wedding service was conducted by Franklin's old headmaster from Groton, the Reverend Endicott Peabody. "Cousin Teddy"—who was now president of the United States—gave Eleanor away, and afterward said to the bridegroom, "Well, Franklin, there's nothing like keeping the name in the family."

Sara, who on the death of her husband had become a very rich woman, later bought a house for the couple in New York. But she also bought an adjoining house for herself, and had the two houses directly connected by sliding doors. Eleanor found herself having to put up with a domineering mother-in-law. This was a very difficult situation for her, but she endured it for the sake of Franklin and her marriage.

▶ *Once Eleanor and Franklin were married, children quickly followed. Here, Eleanor poses for a photograph with Elliott (in her lap), James (left), and Anna (right).*

Job No   :CG 02-008   Trim Size   :W 187 mm X H 229 mm
Job Title:20th Century History Maker Roosevelt   Paper Stock : Matt Art

A Career in Politics

After graduating from Harvard, Franklin Roosevelt was accepted as a student at Columbia Law School in New York. Roosevelt passed his bar exams in 1907 and went to work for the important law firm of Carter, Ledyard, and Milburn, which was based in the financial center of Wall Street.

In his first year, the work was unpaid, but this was not a problem for the Roosevelts as their own private incomes were more than enough to live on.

While Roosevelt worked at his legal career, Eleanor gave birth to a succession of children. Anna was born in 1906 and James the following year. Franklin Jr. was born in 1909, but died shortly afterward of pneumonia—a tragic death that affected both parents. The next child was Elliott, born in 1910. A fourth child was born in 1914 and became the second Franklin Jr.; their fifth, and last was John, born in 1916. For Eleanor this was hard work, and she half-jokingly complained that she was "always getting over a baby or having one." Eleanor was not a natural mother, and the constant, hovering presence of her mother-in-law made life even more difficult for her. During their early years, the children were looked after by English nannies.

Roosevelt found the work of a Wall Street lawyer rather dull, and he soon began to look toward politics as a means of escape from the routine of office life. His chance came in 1910, when the Democratic Party asked him to run for state senator from Columbia, Dutchess, and Putman counties. The voters of this strongly agricultural area normally voted for the Republican Party, and the Democrats were thought to have little chance of success. However, because Roosevelt had a well-known name (and was wealthy enough to pay his own election expenses) and was a local figure

▶ *A portrait of Roosevelt at the beginning of his political career, circa 1910.*

As Franklin's career began to take off, the Roosevelt family relished their visits to their summer home—shown here—on Campobello Island.

(Hyde Park is in Duchess County), it was thought he might have a slim chance of success.

Roosevelt threw himself into the campaign with great enthusiasm. He toured the district in a bright red open-topped car, speaking to the local farmers at every opportunity. He picked up the skills of a good public speaker and averaged about 10 speeches a day. His campaign was based on support for agricultural issues and honest state government—and to the surprise of most people, he won the election by 1,000 votes. The Roosevelt family moved from New York City to the state capital of Albany, and Franklin began life as a politician.

Reactions to Roosevelt

To other Democrats—especially the progressives who worked to improve the conditions of the ordinary working class—Roosevelt was considered to be aloof and uncaring. One major problem for Roosevelt at this time was that his support for the farmers brought him into conflict with the progressive Democrats, who were trying to introduce a bill that would limit the working week for women to 54 hours. Many women worked in canning factories run by New York farmers; the farmers were against the bill, fearing that it would slow down the canning operation and cost them money. Although Roosevelt eventually supported the bill, he had disappointed some of his Democrat colleagues.

One young Democratic reformer who backed the bill was Frances Perkins, and she was not impressed by the dashing young Roosevelt, she found him lacking in sympathy and she disliked some of his mannerisms: "He had an unfortunate habit—so natural that he was unaware of it—of throwing his head up. This, combined with his pince-nez [glasses] and great height, gave him an appearance of looking down his nose at most people." In time, however, Perkins and Roosevelt would become close colleagues.

Fighting Tammany Hall

As senator for a rural district in upstate New York, Roosevelt found himself in conflict with the New York Democratic Party organization called "Tammany Hall," which was considered by many to be corrupt. Roosevelt came up against New York City's top Democrats, including "Big Tim" Sullivan, who called Roosevelt an "awful, arrogant fellow." But Roosevelt loved political battles, even if they were with his own party. He told a reporter, "I've never had as much fun in my life as I am having right now." Although in the end Roosevelt and his supporters were unable to beat the party machine at Tammany Hall, he caught the attention of Democrats throughout the country, many praising him for his spirited fight.

Howe Joins Roosevelt

In 1912 Roosevelt ran for a second term as a New York state senator, but before he could start his election campaign he was struck down by typhoid fever and confined to bed. Fortunately for the Roosevelt campaign, a veteran newspaper reporter named Louis McHenry Howe offered his services. Like Perkins, he had not particularly liked Roosevelt at first. He called him "a silk-pants sort of guy," but he admired his spirit and thought he had the potential to succeed at the highest level.

Howe fought a brilliant campaign for Roosevelt, distributing an avalanche of posters, leaflets, and letters to bring out support. Roosevelt won without appearing in public once. Howe would stay with Roosevelt and become an essential part of his political machine in the years to come, providing sound advice and encouragement, especially when things went against his boss.

Support for Wilson Pays Off

During the 1912 presidential election campaign, Roosevelt had vigorously supported Woodrow Wilson, the Democratic candidate. Wilson was nominated and won the presidential election, and as a reward he offered Roosevelt the post of Assistant Secretary of the U.S. Navy. Roosevelt happily accepted this great leap into a full government position. His interest in the sea and naval matters made him a good choice for the job. He wrote, "All my life I have loved ships and been a student of the navy." Interestingly, this very post had been held by former president Theodore Roosevelt, and Franklin saw this as an omen of good luck, because he hoped to follow "Cousin Teddy" to the highest office in the land.

In 1913 Roosevelt left New York and traveled south with his family, to begin his new job in Washington, D.C.

▶ *President Woodrow Wilson offered Roosevelt the job of Assistant Secretary of the Navy.*

War and Political Defeat

Roosevelt had lost none of his enthusiasm for a new project, and he proved to be a most energetic and effective assistant secretary.

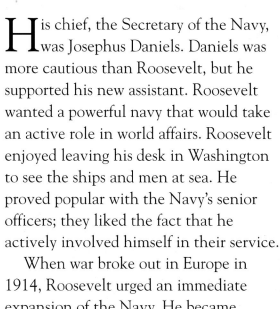

German U-boats (submarines) caused havoc during World War I, sinking thousands of ships.

His chief, the Secretary of the Navy, was Josephus Daniels. Daniels was more cautious than Roosevelt, but he supported his new assistant. Roosevelt wanted a powerful navy that would take an active role in world affairs. Roosevelt enjoyed leaving his desk in Washington to see the ships and men at sea. He proved popular with the Navy's senior officers; they liked the fact that he actively involved himself in their service.

When war broke out in Europe in 1914, Roosevelt urged an immediate expansion of the Navy. He became convinced that the United States should become involved in the war on the side of the Allies (led by Britain and France) against Germany, whose U-boats (submarines) had sunk a number of American ships in the Atlantic. Once the U.S. declared war on Germany in 1917, Roosevelt traveled to Europe where he inspected American ships and even visited the front-line trenches near the French position of Verdun.

Roosevelt put forward several proposals to defeat the German submarine menace. One of his more successful was the North Sea Mine Barrage. Although his superiors,

27

including Daniels, thought it was impractical, he managed to convince President Wilson to go ahead with the idea. This involved the British and U.S. navies laying some 70,000 underwater mines between northern Scotland and Norway. The intention was to prevent German U-boats from traveling around northern Scotland and into the Atlantic to attack British and American shipping. Although the plan was not finished when the war ended in 1918, it had helped keep the German navy penned within its North Sea bases.

An Expanding Navy

Roosevelt had played an important part in the huge wartime expansion of the U.S. Navy from just under 200 ships to over 2,000. It was a tremendous achievement, and it brought him respect from both the Navy and the government. Roosevelt also gained valuable experience in administering a government department, and he developed many political contacts in Washington and within the Democratic Party.

When President Wilson traveled to Paris to attend the Versailles Peace Conference (held at the end of World War I), Roosevelt went with him. Wilson was horrified by the war, and he believed that the major countries should band together in a League of Nations to prevent a world war from ever happening again. Roosevelt supported Wilson, but the U.S. Congress did not want the country to become involved in European affairs and refused to let the United States join the League of Nations.

Growing Influence

Roosevelt's growing influence within the Democratic Party was helped by his reconciliation with the "Tammany Hall" machine in his native New York. He did not challenge the power or interfere with the workings of Tammany Hall again, and, for their part, they "forgave and forgot" what they saw as his youthful indiscretions. Roosevelt was now a rising star in the Party, and for the 1920 presidential elections he was asked to be the running mate (vice president) of Democratic presidential candidate James M. Cox, the Governor of Ohio. Roosevelt was now 38 and had become an effective and likeable public speaker.

▶ *Roosevelt as Assistant Secretary of the Navy with his boss, Secretary Josephus Daniels.*

Formerly, the vice-presidential candidate took a back seat in the election campaign, but Roosevelt was a tireless campaigner: he visited 32 states and made over 1,000 speeches. Despite his best efforts, however, the tide of politics had turned against the Democrats in favor of the Republican Party. The Democrats wanted the United States to play a full part in international affairs, in contrast to the position held by Republican candidate Warren G. Harding and his running mate Calvin Coolidge. They were called isolationists, as they believed the United States should withdraw (or isolate itself) from world affairs and concentrate on developing the home economy.

▼ *President Woodrow Wilson (center) and other delegates at Versailles in June 1919. French prime minister Georges Clemenceau is on Wilson's left.*

Defeat and Private Turmoil

The American people wanted change: they had become disillusioned with the Democrats, and many agreed with the Republicans and liked their promise of a "return to normalcy." Harding won by a wide margin, taking 37 of the (then) 48 states. The Republicans also won control of both houses of Congress—the House of Representatives and the Senate. Throughout the 1920s the Republicans would dominate the political life of America.

Although obviously disappointed by the outcome of the election, Roosevelt was not downcast. He had gained valuable experience campaigning at a national level, and his name was now well known throughout the country. Always an optimist, Roosevelt explained, "The moment of defeat is the best time to lay plans for future victories."

Roosevelt's roller coaster ride in politics was matched by turmoil at home. While living in Washington, Franklin and Eleanor had grown apart; whereas he liked the parties and social life that went with his job as Assistant Secretary of the Navy, Eleanor's natural shyness made things difficult for her. Also, Roosevelt was spending long periods away from home on official government business. It was during this time that Roosevelt had a romantic affair with Lucy Mercer, a young woman who had once worked as Eleanor's social

▲ Lucy Mercer, with whom Roosevelt had a romantic affair. The incident nearly cost him his marriage.

secretary. When Eleanor found out about the affair, she was devastated. Eleanor wrote, "The bottom dropped out of my world. I faced myself, my surroundings, my world, honestly for the first time." She confronted her husband and offered him two choices: either they would continue the marriage for the children's sake and he must break off with Lucy Mercer, or, in her words, she would "give him his freedom" to divorce her.

At that time divorce was considered a scandal, and it probably would have wrecked Roosevelt's career. He was unsure what to do, but his mother and his trusted aide Louis Howe convinced him that he must continue his career as a politician and give up this relationship. He eventually accepted, and the affair was brought to a halt. Although the marriage continued, there were lasting scars. But Eleanor always stood by her husband, and over time she became one of his most trusted political advisors. Their relationship now became a working partnership—and a very successful one at that.

◀ *Warren G. Harding, who won the 1920 presidential election.*

Resuming Private Life

After the election Roosevelt left Washington for New York, where he resumed his legal career. He set up a law partnership called Emmet, Marvin, and Roosevelt and was appointed vice president of a bonding firm called the Fidelity & Deposit Company. The work was not too difficult and he had spare time to devote to other activities, which included charity work for the blind and the Boy Scouts as well as keeping in touch with the political world.

Disaster Strikes

In the summer of 1921, the Roosevelt family went on vacation to Campobello Island. Roosevelt needed a rest after years of hard political campaigning, and the recent presidential elections had been more exhausting than he realized.

After a day's sailing, Roosevelt and his three elder children, Anna, James, and Elliott, went for a two mile jog and a swim in the cold waters off New Brunswick. When they returned, Roosevelt felt ill: he thought he had a bad cold and went to bed.

The next morning he had a severe fever and difficulty moving his legs. The pain spread to his neck and back, and soon he lost all ability to move his legs. Local doctors had no idea what the problem was, but when a specialist was called in he correctly diagnosed that Roosevelt had contracted the terrible viral disease of polio (poliomyelitis), which would leave him paralyzed from the waist down.

Roosevelt spent the autumn of 1921 in a hospital in New York. Every attempt was made to get his legs to work again, but eventually it became clear that he would not be able to walk without assistance. He was fitted with steel braces, which ran from his hips to his feet, and he could walk only with the aid of crutches. Despite this, Roosevelt refused to give up hope that someday he might walk unaided again, and he spent hours improving his skill with crutches.

Despite his best efforts to find some sort of "cure" for polio, his legs became limp and lifeless. But inside, his spirit grew; he became a bigger and better person. Roosevelt's aide Louis Howe described this change: "His thoughts expanded, his horizon widened. He began to see the other fellow's point of view. He thought of others who were ill and inflicted and in want." Eleanor Roosevelt also wrote of the change in Roosevelt's character: "[He] had to think out the

FDR and Polio

For such an active person as Roosevelt, the onset of polio was a terrible blow. He showed great courage in the way he refused to let this crippling disease take over his life. He would sometimes joke about his polio, ending a conversation with a cheery, "Goodbye, I've got to run."

fundamentals of living and learn the greatest of all lessons—infinite patience and never-ending persistence."

While Roosevelt struggled with his illness, his mother and Eleanor fought over his future. Sara wanted her son to retire from politics and live the life of a country gentleman at Hyde Park. Eleanor, however, was determined that her husband should continue his legal and political activities. There were quarrels between the two women. Assisted by Louis Howe, however, Eleanor prevailed and Roosevelt returned to work with the Fidelity & Deposit Company in 1922. He also kept in touch with the political scene.

In 1924 he supported the Governor of New York, Alfred E. Smith, in his attempt to become the presidential nominee

◀ *After recovering from polio, Roosevelt had to wear braces on his legs, as seen here in this rare view.*

of the Democratic Party. Although Smith failed, people were aware that Roosevelt was back—his speech, made on crutches, to the Democratic Convention in New York was a personal triumph. The *New York Herald Tribune* congratulated him: "Franklin D. Roosevelt stands out as the real hero of the Democratic Convention."

Warm Springs

In his search to find a cure for polio, Roosevelt came across a down-at-the-heels health spa in Georgia called Warm Springs. He found the warm medicinal waters at the spa a great help, even though no cure was found. In 1926 Roosevelt bought Warm Springs and spent large amounts of money improving the facilities, turning it into a treatment center for polio sufferers from all over the world. Roosevelt would regularly visit Warm Springs for the rest of his life.

While Roosevelt was staying at Warm Springs in 1928, he was asked by Alfred E. Smith to run for Smith's old job: Governor of New York. Smith had been nominated by the Democrats to be their candidate for the 1928 presidential elections, and he wanted the powerful Roosevelt name to make sure that the vitally important state of New York would remain under Democrat control. Roosevelt and his advisors wanted him to stay out of the contest: Eleanor thought he should continue to build up his strength, and Louis Howe argued that, as the Democrats would almost certainly do badly in the 1928 elections, Roosevelt should keep his head down until the next round of presidential elections in 1932.

Campaigning for Governor

But Smith finally wore down Roosevelt's reluctance to run, and he put his name forward for governor. The first hurdle Roosevelt faced was to convince the voters that he was fit enough to do the job. As in the past, he traveled through New York State speaking to the crowds. He often delivered his speeches from the back of an open-topped car, so that his disability was not so apparent. He enjoyed the campaign, telling a friend, "It's rare good fun to be back in action. I had almost forgotten the thrill of it."

▶ *Roosevelt attempted to find a "cure" for polio at Warm Springs spa, in Georgia. Here he fishes from an open boat. Although a poor-quality photograph, his emaciated legs and braces are clearly visible.*

Democratic Defeat

The Republicans were the stronger party, and under Herbert Hoover they won the presidential election by a landslide. The Democrats suffered one of their most humiliating defeats, but in the New York State governor's race, Roosevelt was able to turn the tables and narrowly defeat his Republican opponent, Albert Ottinger.

Roosevelt was sworn in as governor on January 1, 1929, exactly 30 years after Theodore Roosevelt had been sworn in to the same post. Their careers were closely tied together: both men had been assistant secretaries of the Navy before becoming governors of New York. Theodore had gone on to become president of the United States. Would Franklin follow him to the ultimate job in American politics?

▶ *Roosevelt was elected governor of New York in 1928 and 1930. Here he is at his swearing-in ceremony, with Eleanor to his left.*

From New York to the White House

Roosevelt proved so great a success as Governor of New York that when elections occurred again in 1930 for a second term of two years, he won by a landslide.

Roosevelt was unusual among New York politicians in being able to draw upon the loyalties of the city-dwellers of New York as well as the farmers of rural upstate New York, where he had once been a senator.

While he was governor, Roosevelt gathered around him a team of gifted people to help him run New York State. As well as his trusted aide Louis Howe, his team included James Farley, Frances Perkins, and Samuel Rosenman, who were all to play an important role in the years to come. And there was always Eleanor, who had now come out of his shadow, and was doing her own work in the field of social welfare.

The Republican Party was the dominant force in American political life throughout the 1920s, and Roosevelt and the Democrats found it hard to match

A Liberal Democrat

Roosevelt was a "liberal" type of Democrat, which meant that he believed government—whether state or federal—should take an active role in people's lives and that business should be regulated. Among his measures were the introduction of state-supported old-age pensions, an unemployment insurance plan (which paid out money to those out of work), and laws that prevented women and children from having to work excessively long hours. Roosevelt also helped the agricultural community by cutting taxes for small farmers and providing funds for rural education. He also became something of an early conservationist by encouraging the planting of forests. These policies did mean that taxes had to go up, however, and this made him unpopular with the better-off, who had to pay more.

▶ *A bustling New York street scene from the late 1920s.*

them. Republicans believed that the government should not interfere in industry and business. The prosperity that much of America enjoyed during this decade seemed to prove the Republicans right. Unemployment was low and for the majority of people living standards were rising. New consumer goods—such as automobiles, radios, and kitchen appliances—were now being bought by all but the poorest people, and if they couldn't afford to buy them outright, they paid for them in monthly instalments. The stock market was booming, and people invested money in stocks and shares when they saw their values rapidly increasing.

The "Crash"

The American economy looked very strong, especially as industrial and agricultural output grew. But this prosperity was built on shaky foundations, and the collapse, which began in 1929, had disastrous consequences for the American people. On October 24, prices on the New York Stock Exchange suddenly plunged, and by the end of the

◀ After the "boom" years of the 1920s, the stock market crash was a terrible shock. The sign on this expensive car says it all.

month they had collapsed. The financial district of Wall Street was gripped by panic, as people began to sell all their shares. But millions of shares had become worthless and could not be sold. Not only did many investors lose all their money, they found themselves in debt because they had borrowed money to invest on the stock exchange.

From Boom to Bust

The Wall Street crash was followed by an economic slump: people stopped buying goods, firms went bankrupt, and workers found themselves without jobs. Industry in America had begun to experience problems before October 1929, but the disaster on the New York Stock Exchange made things much worse. Another problem was the unregulated American banking system. Banks had loaned out too much money, so that when worried investors suddenly asked for their money back, the banks were unable to pay them. As a result, financial institutions throughout the country went bankrupt, causing mayhem.

President Herbert Hoover told America that the economic crisis would not last long, and that people should stay calm. He firmly believed that the government should stay out of the crisis. But things just got worse. In 1929 there was hardly any unemployment at all, but by 1931 eight million Americans were out of work, and by 1933 the figure had grown to over 12 million, representing at least 25 percent unemployment. In some major cities the figure was much higher, nearing 50 percent.

Everybody suffered. The farmers and people who worked on the land found that prices had dropped so much that their crops were sometimes not worth harvesting, and so they were allowed to rot in the soil. The slump extended to all jobs and professions, hitting both the working and middle classes. And for those still employed, wages fell rapidly— far faster than store prices.

Effects of the Slump

To make matters worse, the U.S. was the only major industrialized country not to have a nationwide system of unemployment and poverty relief. Previously, people falling on hard times relied on their families and local charities for help. These were now completely out of their depth, and by the early 1930s millions of people had been thrown into abject poverty. The effects of the Great Depression were devastating. Marriages and birth rates plunged as young Americans rejected the possibility of raising families, and between 1929 and 1932 the suicide rate rose by almost a quarter. There were a few cases where families were so short of food that parents even killed their own children rather than see them starve.

▼ *The effects of the slump were disastrous. Here, unemployed people line up for free food.*

45

Job No   : CG 02-008
Job Title: 20th Century History Maker Roosevelt
Client   : The Watt Group

Trim Size   : W 187 mm X H 229 mm
Paper Stock : Mat...
Screen

When the Depression first started, Roosevelt followed the traditional line, which said that the laws of supply and demand would sort out the problem. As the crisis deepened, however, he realized that direct action was needed. In his state of New York—which had a million people out of work—Roosevelt introduced the Temporary Emergency Relief Administration (TERA) in August 1931. Funded by the state, TERA provided food, clothing, and shelter to those in need, and helped the unemployed look for work. This was the first time a state administration had ever intervened in this way to help the unemployed. However, the cost of this intervention doubled the rate of state income tax.

The Road to the White House

As early as 1930, just after winning his second term as Governor of New York, Roosevelt had made the decision to run for the Democratic nomination in the 1932 presidential elections. Although he faced some stiff opposition, his reputation as a man who made things happen ensured he was the most attractive and

A scene from the 1932 presidential election.

dynamic candidate, and he won on the fourth ballot. Breaking with tradition, Roosevelt flew to the Democratic Convention in Chicago to accept the nomination—candidates had previously been informed of their victory at home. In his acceptance speech, he famously told the delegates: "I pledge you, I pledge myself, to a new deal for the American people." Although he did not outline his policies in any detail, his campaign during the autumn of 1932 inspired hope in a people who were desperate for some alternative to Hoover's "wait-and-see"

▲ *Roosevelt speaks to the crowds from the rear carriage of his train during the 1932 campaign.*

policy. Roosevelt toured the country in a special train, stopping at every station to address the crowds.

The American people liked Roosevelt's optimistic message, and he convincingly defeated Hoover in the November elections, winning 42 of the 48 states. The Democrats also won large majorities in both houses of Congress. On hearing of his victory, Roosevelt said, "This is the greatest night of my life!" But the ultimate test was about to begin.

The First New Deal

In the period between Roosevelt's winning the 1932 election in November and his inauguration as President of the United States in March 1933, America's economic crisis got even worse.

Unemployment was increasing—as many as two million people were wandering the country looking for work, and hundreds of thousands were forced to live in shacks and tents nicknamed "Hoovervilles"—after the former President Hoover. And another banking crisis was sweeping the country: 38 states had closed their banks as depositors desperately tried to take out money the banks did not have. During this time, Roosevelt organized his team to prepare for action after his inauguration on March 4. At his inaugural speech, he tried to reassure the nation, saying: "The only thing we have to fear is fear itself." He went on to say that he would not stand by and let the Depression get worse, that the American people would get "action and action now" and that "our primary task is to put people to work." It was a rousing speech made to a vast crowd of 100,000 people in Washington and broadcast to the nation by radio.

Roosevelt took many of his old political advisors from his New York days to the White House. His first cabinet included Cordell Hull (Secretary of State), Frances Perkins (Secretary for Labor—and the first ever female cabinet member), James Farley (Postmaster General), and Harold L. Ikes (Secretary of the Interior). FDR's political mentor Louis Howe remained a personal advisor. But this was not to last long. Howe died in 1935, and the Roosevelt administration lost one of its most faithful supporters.

Once in office, Roosevelt immediately set about restoring the nation's confidence in the banking system. He shut all the nation's banks, declaring a four-day "bank holiday." The new Emergency Banking Relief Act allowed the federal government to examine the accounts of every bank. Only the stronger banks would be allowed to reopen and

▶ *President-elect Roosevelt's inauguration on March 4, 1933.*

50

Job No :CG 02-008
Job Title:20th Century History Maker Roosevelt
Client :The Watt Group

Trim Size :W 187 mm X H 22
Paper Stock : Matt Art
Screen : #150 **Colour:**5c

do business; the others would be managed by government agents until their futures could be decided.

A New Approach

Roosevelt addressed the nation over the radio, explaining in straightforward, simple terms what he had done and why. He urged people to return their money to the newly reopened banks, promising them that they were a safer place for their money than being hidden under the mattress. Roosevelt's plea worked, and Americans began to line up to return money instead of taking it out. Within a week, 75 percent of banks were open for business. This broadcast was the first of Roosevelt's radio "fireside chats." They became a regular means of talking to the people—who much appreciated this farsighted and direct approach.

Another feature of the Roosevelt administration were the regular press conferences held in the White House. Previously, journalists had had to submit written questions in advance, but Roosevelt held open sessions in a relaxed

◄ *Frances Perkins, Secretary of Labor, pictured with Peter Fraser, the prime minister of New Zealand, at a labor conference in Philadelphia.*

manner and allowed the press to ask any question they liked. Roosevelt clearly enjoyed the give-and-take of these sessions—as did the journalists. For their part, the journalists were asked not to take photographs of Roosevelt's disability and not to ask questions about it. This was a request that was honored throughout his entire time as president.

The New Deal

Taking its name from a phrase in Roosevelt's acceptance speech at the Democratic Convention, the New Deal was an attempt to get America and its people back to work and achieve some degree of prosperity. As had been the case during his time as Governor of New York, Roosevelt made good use of special advisors to help him deal with the desperate problems faced by the nation. This "think tank" included some of the most respected professional economists and university professors. Many bright young minds also experienced their first taste of government in Washington, D.C. during these years.

The opening phase of Roosevelt's presidency—called the 100 Days—saw a great number of new laws put before and passed by Congress, which were the foundation of the New Deal. In their haste, they were sometimes chaotic and occasionally contradicted each other, but they backed up the president's promise to act. They were later dubbed "The Three Rs"—Relief, Recovery, and Reform.

Under the leadership of Harry Hopkins, the Federal Emergency Relief Administration took $500 million of federal government money to provide food and clothes for the unemployed; by 1935 a further $1.5 billion had been spent in direct grants and work relief. A host of agencies came into being almost overnight, usually known by their initials (Roosevelt himself was now called FDR).

The "Alphabet" Agencies

Among the first of the "alphabet" agencies was the Civilian Conservation Corps (CCC), which employed young men to carry out conservation work such as fighting fires, planting trees, and creating wildlife refuges. They were paid a small wage and given food and clothing, and when the plan ended in 1942 some 2.5 million men had passed through the CCC. The Public Works Administration (PWA) used the unemployed in other

▶ *Roosevelt created a new and popular presidential style, broadcasting over the radio to the nation from the White House.*

public works projects, building roads, bridges, hospitals, and houses. In the field of economic recovery, the New Deal was less successful. The National Recovery Administration (NRA) was an attempt to regulate the world of business and create greater trust between management and the workers. The NRA encouraged the establishment of codes of fair competition within each industry. Prices and production were regulated, minimum wages and maximum hours were set, while the worker's trade or labor unions were given the right to bargain for better conditions. Unfortunately, in trying to please everybody, the NRA ended up pleasing nobody. Many (mainly bigger) industries found ways to bypass the regulations; smaller businesses claimed the rules were unfair; and the unions grumbled that labor guarantees were being undercut.

The Agricultural Adjustment Administration (AAA) was designed to promote recovery in rural areas. At the time of the crash, farms were producing too much food, and after the crash prices

completely collapsed. The main objective of the AAA was to raise the prices of food coming from farms. This was to be achieved by giving farmers subsidy payments to cut the amount of food produced, so that prices would eventually rise. In some respects the AAA was successful: in Roosevelt's first term, farm incomes rose by 50 percent. However, rising prices meant that poor people in urban areas could not afford decent food.

The TVA Plan

The physically most dramatic of the New Deal plans was the institution of the Tennessee Valley Authority (TVA) in 1933. The Tennessee River Valley was a large area that comprised parts of seven southern states. The area was one of the poorest in the United States; few people had access to electricity and many people died of disease and malnutrition. It was estimated that up to a million families had to survive on a diet of salt pork and cornmeal. Attempts had been made in the past to dam the Tennessee River, but these had been blocked by private power

◀ *Roosevelt made a point of traveling around the country to meet ordinary Americans. Here he talks to farming families in North Dakota.*

companies who feared for their profits. The TVA was given the power to build 21 dams. This changed the whole economy of the region. The dams generated cheap hydroelectricity and controlled the constant flooding and soil erosion that had blighted farming. As a byproduct, nitrogen fertilizer was produced, which helped increase the quality of crops. As an example of its success, in 1933 less that three percent of farms in the Tennessee Valley had access to electricity; by 1945 this figure had risen to 75 percent.

Protecting Savers

The last of the three "Rs"—reform—consisted mainly of changes to the financial system. The Federal Deposit Insurance Corporation (FDIC) was set up to protect people's savings. This insurance plan allowed savers to get their money back even if a bank collapsed. The plan also increased public confidence in the banking system. The Securities and Exchange Commission (SEC) was set up in 1934, as a first step to regulating the stock market and preventing another Wall Street crash.

A Turning Point

The first phase of the New Deal, which lasted roughly from 1933 to 1935, was a turning point in the history of the United States. FDR and his government halted the slide to economic and social disaster that had occurred during the final years of the Hoover administration. Above all, the American people had been given hope, and the belief that, in time, prosperity would return. But even after two years of the New Deal, unemployment had been reduced only by a fairly small amount (from 13 to 11 million), and Roosevelt was being criticized from both the left and right of the political spectrum. Left-wingers thought he had not gone far enough to transform the economic system, while those on the right criticized him for intervening too much in the economy and throttling the spirit of free enterprise. But Roosevelt's supporters argued that to turn around an economy took time, and it was still too early to judge whether the New Deal was working or not.

▶ Roosevelt inspects a great 1930s building project, the Boulder Dam in Nevada. Now called the Hoover Dam, it was built between 1931–1935.

Life in the White House

To the many visitors who went to the White House in the 1930s, one of the most surprising things was the relaxed attitude of the president himself.

Roosevelt was a genial man with a sunny temperament, and even when things were going badly for the government he always had a smile or jovial comment.

He was a man who liked people, and even those who disagreed with Roosevelt on political lines admitted that it was hard not to like him—especially when you knew him on a personal level. For the many millions of ordinary Americans hit hard by the Great Depression, FDR gave them a feeling that he understood and empathized with their problems; he came to be seen as a personal friend.

When his first inaugural speech was broadcast to the nation, he received nearly half-a-million letters from the public. One person wrote: "Your human feelings for all of us in your address is just wonderful." Throughout his presidency, Roosevelt received a vast mail bag— between 5,000 and 8,000 people wrote to him every day, most thanking him for his help and encouragement.

The White House became a hive of activity, but FDR set an informal tone. His children invited friends to stay, and in the mornings his grandchildren would burst into his bedroom and jump around on his bed. And there would always be a constant stream of visitors arriving to meet the President.

The presidential day would begin with Roosevelt eating his breakfast in bed, while working on government business or reading a selection of newspapers. Between 10 and 10:30 A.M., he was taken to his downstairs office, and there began to meet his visitors, who would normally be given 15 minutes to talk to the President—although if he liked what they

▼ *The White House—a picture from the 1930s.*

had to say, time could easily overrun. He ate lunch at his desk, and he would continue to do business as he ate. After working through the afternoon, Roosevelt left his office at around 5:30 P.M. and would then relax, often with a swim in the White House pool (he believed that water was helpful in fighting polio).

Dinner was at 9 P.M., after a round of cocktails, and the rest of the evening was usually taken up with one of his many pastimes and hobbies. He enjoyed playing cards with friends and colleagues. Poker was a favorite game and he was especially delighted when he beat vice-president John Nance Garner, reckoned to be one of the best poker players in Washington.

▶ *"Another hot dog?" As an example of their relaxed and open style, Franklin, Eleanor, and Franklin, Jr. enjoy a picnic—and invite photographers along.*

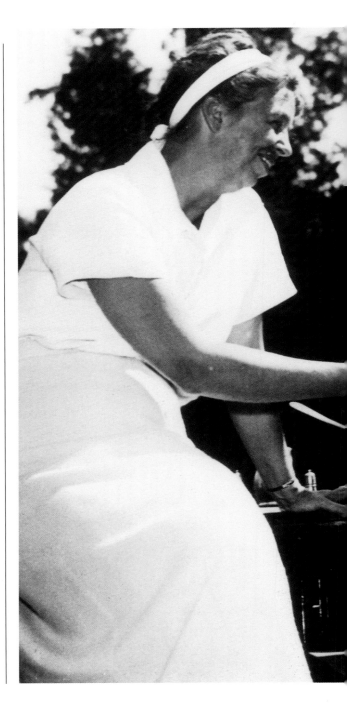

If he was alone, he might spend time in the painstaking construction of model sailing ships, or in sorting out his extensive stamp collection. In fact, Roosevelt was such a stamp enthusiast that the U.S. Post Office Department sent him copies of all their first editions as a matter of course.

Roosevelt was also a big baseball fan, and he enjoyed the presidential custom of throwing out the opening ball of the season. He wrote, "I am the kind of fan who wants to get plenty of action for his money." When he had more time, Roosevelt would slip away from the White House and relax back at home in Hyde Park, or go south to Georgia and enjoy the waters at Warm Springs. He also kept up his passion for the sea and sailed his boat off the coast of New England. Roosevelt was the sort of man who knew how to work and relax, and both were important while he was trying to put the nation back on its feet.

Hardworking Eleanor

Besides his cabinet and advisors, Roosevelt increasingly relied upon Eleanor to act as his "eyes and ears." His lack of mobility prevented him from going to the sorts of places that Eleanor was able to visit. She would inspect hospitals, factories, slum housing projects, and even coal mines. This sort of activity was unheard of for the White House's "first lady," but Eleanor was determined to make her mark. Their youngest son, John, wrote of his parents, "They were a team, and the Roosevelt years, I believe, were more fruitful and creative as a consequence of that partnership." As well as acting as her husband's "private investigator," Eleanor traveled around the country in her own right, and wrote up what she saw and thought in a daily newspaper column called "My Day," which was read across America.

Eleanor was a much more radical person than FDR, and she had a major influence on him in convincing him of the need to support women and America's black population, which suffered continuing social, political, and economic injustice. She encouraged him to employ both women and blacks in more senior positions in the White House and in the many agencies created by the New Deal. Although these were still only small steps toward greater equality for all citizens of the United States, at the time they seemed like dramatic advances for a president to make.

▶ *Roosevelt's interest in stamp collecting was one that he pursued throughout his life.*

63

Job No   :CG 02-008
Job Title:20th Century History Maker Roosevelt
Client   :The Watt Group

Trim Size   :W 187 mm X H 229 mm
Paper Stock : M-
Screen

The Second New Deal

After the flurry of new laws that had been passed
in 1933 during the "first hundred days,"
there was a slowdown in the New Deal.

Job No   :CG 02-008
Job Title :20th Century History Maker Roosevelt
Client   :The Watt Group

Trim Size   :W 187 mm X H 22
Paper Stock : Matt Art
Screen   : #150   Colour:5c

Then in the summer of 1935, Roosevelt introduced a further series of new laws to the U.S. Congress, later called the Second New Deal. Some historians have seen this new round of lawmaking as a move toward the political left, but if there was any such movement it was very slight. Roosevelt always maintained that he only wanted to reform the American capitalist system—to make it more efficient and more humane—and not replace it whole-scale with something different.

Three significant laws were passed by Congress in 1935. The first was the creation of the Works Progress Administration (WPA). This was another plan to provide the unemployed with basic payments for work on public projects. As many as eight million people were involved in this wide-ranging program.

As well as the construction of roads, bridges, hospitals, and schools, the WPA served hot meals to schoolchildren and encouraged the unemployed to continue their education.

Another feature of the WPA was the involvement of artists, writers, photographers, and musicians. They went out into the country to paint murals in public buildings, to record the stories of the poor (including accounts from the last ex-slaves) or to produce plays and musical works for audiences who had never been to a theater or concert hall.

◀ The 1930s were a time of civil turmoil throughout the United States and clashes were common. Here, police break up a communist demonstration in Los Angeles, February 1931.

Social Security

The most influential of the three new laws, and at the time the most controversial, was the introduction of social security. While most European nations had developed social security systems, which acted as a safety net for those fallen on hard times, it was virtually unknown in America. The Social Security Act of August 1935 provided payment for pensioners and the disabled, and unemployment insurance for those without work—they would receive payments while they looked for jobs. The payments were small and only about half of the work force were eligible. At first, opposition to the plan was intense. Opponents said it would undermine the traditional American virtue of "self-help," but its popularity with the vast majority of the less well-off won the day.

The second measure was the passing of the Wagner Act in 1935. This set up the National Labor Relations Board (NLRB), which gave to the unions legal protection and the right to bargain with management, who were not allowed to prevent workers from joining unions.

Opponents of the New Deal

Most political resistance to Roosevelt and the New Deal came from the political right. They disapproved of FDR's spending on social reform, which led to higher taxes for those who were better off and increased borrowing by the federal government (which increased the national debt). But there were others from the left who thought Roosevelt had failed to seize an opportunity to transform America. Most of these were either socialists or communists, but there were other critics who enjoyed great popularity at the time.

The Reverend Charles E. Coughlin, the "radio priest," had started off as a New Deal supporter but later broke with Roosevelt. In his own radio broadcasts, which for a period had up to 40 million listeners, he bitterly and bizarrely denounced Roosevelt as a "double-crossing" supporter of godless capitalists, communists, and international bankers.

Another strange figure was a California doctor named Francis E. Townsend, who argued that everyone over 60 should be given a pension of $200 a month, provided the money was spent in that month—the idea being to increase the nation's purchasing power and encourage industrial production. The third maverick was Huey "Kingfish" Long, a senator from Louisiana who started the Share-Our-Wealth campaign, which by 1935 had millions of supporters. But Long was assassinated by a political rival in 1935, and his movement, along with those of Coughlin and Townsend, collapsed as quickly as it had begun.

The New Deal program met its stiffest opposition from the Supreme Court, the third branch of federal government, one of whose functions was to ensure that new laws did not break the terms of the United States Constitution. During early 1935 the Supreme Court began to attack much New Deal legislation, arguing that the federal government had no right to

▶ *Rev. Charles E. Coughlin makes one of his broadcasts.*

exercise such powers over individual state governments. The Court eventually ruled that the NRA and AAA were illegal. Not only was Roosevelt infuriated by this decision, he was also fearful that the Supreme Court would block other acts, including the TVA, the Social Security Act, and the Wagner Act.

A New Election

The next round of presidential elections in 1936 gave Roosevelt a chance to let the nation decide who was right. He campaigned in his usual energetic manner, crisscrossing the country in the presidential express train, and argued that the "we have only just begun to fight" to improve the conditions of the "forgotten man." Big business was against Roosevelt but the nation was for him, and he won the most resounding victory in American politics since 1820. He took 61 percent of the popular vote, and gained all but two of the 48 states of the union.

With this magnificent victory behind him, FDR felt inspired to carry on the fight for the New Deal with renewed vigor. In his inaugural address he

◀ Senator Huey "Kingfish" Long also opposed the New Deal. He was assassinated in 1935.

reminded America that much still had to be done, and that a third of the nation was still "ill-housed, ill-clad, and ill-nourished." But almost immediately, Roosevelt came up against the Supreme Court, so that by the beginning of 1937 the Court had blocked 11 out of 17 of his programs. Roosevelt took on the Supreme Court, and he proposed to increase the number of judges from nine to 15. This proposal caused uproar within the entire American political system. As the defender of the Constitution, the Supreme Court was considered to be above everyday politics, and Roosevelt was accused of trying to "pack" the Supreme Court with judges who were supporters of the New Deal. Even some Democrats opposed the plan, and Roosevelt suffered the humiliation of a Democratic dominated Congress voting down his proposal.

This was Roosevelt's first major defeat as President, a setback that tarnished his image as an honest and fair politician. Ironically, the Supreme Court subsequently began to support New Deal measures, and with the appointment of a new judge (after one had retired), the

▲ *FDR and Eleanor leave a wedding at Hyde Park on July 20, 1936. Eleanor was always forthright about publicly expressing her views and opinions, as is evident here from the expression on her face.*

Court and Roosevelt were no longer at odds.

The biggest practical consequence of this whole episode was FDR's inability to control the more conservative-minded Democrats. After siding with the Republicans during the Supreme Court fight, their former allegiance to Roosevelt had been broken, and from then on they often sided with the Republicans (who had also made gains in the 1938 Congressional elections) when progressive legislation was being proposed. From 1938 onward, it was Congess—not the Supreme Court—that was the main bar to the progress of New Deal laws.

Labor Unrest

Further problems affected Roosevelt's second term as President. The Wagner Act of 1935 had allowed workers to join the union of their choice, but when they took up this right in large numbers during 1937–1938, they were opposed by the big manufacturers who were often violently antiunion. The workers hoped to improve their working conditions, and they organized a number of strikes and industrial sit-ins.

▼ *Strikers picket car giant General Motors during the strike of 1937.*

Violence and Intimidation

The big employers responded through intimidation, and used force to break up the strikes. Henry Ford, owner of the great automobile company, used his own private police force to deal with strikers. The industrial unrest led to increased violence between the two sides, which culminated in the Memorial Day "battle" of May 31, 1937. On this occasion, strikers from the Republic Steel Works and police fought running battles that led to ten people being killed and a further 84 injured. Although the President tried to stand apart from these quarrels, both workers and employers (unfairly) blamed him for not taking their side.

▼ *Uniformed police, armed with sticks, move striking Chicago steelworkers on June 8, 1937.*

The Road to War

The difficulties encountered by the Roosevelt government were almost always domestic issues regarding the economy, but from 1937 onward FDR was faced with a new set of problems outside the United States.

Increasingly, the New Deal would be put aside as Roosevelt wrestled with the foreign threats to peace and stability.

Adolf Hitler gained power in Germany in 1933—the same year that FDR first became President—and he immediately set about transforming Germany into a fascist state. Whereas Roosevelt wanted to solve his country's economic problems and improve living conditions for the poor, Hitler was obsessed with the idea of making Germany the most powerful nation in Europe. During the 1930s Germany did become increasingly powerful, breaking diplomatic treaties, bullying smaller states, and threatening war. In 1936 Hitler reoccupied the

▶ *The road to World War II—Adolf Hilter reviews troops in Nuremburg, September 1937.*

demilitarized Rhineland zone. In March 1938 German troops marched into Austria, which was absorbed into the "Greater German Reich"; and later in 1938 Hitler took over important areas of Czechoslovakia.

The new fascist government of Italy, led by the dictator Benito Mussolini, was

also engaged in military conquest, and in 1935 Italian troops invaded Ethiopia, in direct contravention of the League of Nations. The trend toward right-wing dictatorships took place in other European countries, including Finland, Romania, and Spain. On the other side of the world, the growth of Japanese militarism in the 1930s was another factor increasing instability in the world. Short of natural resources, the Japanese decided to acquire them by force, first invading Korea and then China. Wherever they went, the Japanese acted with immense cruelty to the local people they encountered.

Grim Warnings

Germany's increasingly aggressive action in Europe during 1938 and 1939 led Roosevelt to shift his attitude. Instead of acceptance he began to warn the American people of the dangers they faced from a world dominated by dictators. And when Germany invaded Poland in September 1939—the outbreak of World War II—Roosevelt felt he must act. In a "fireside chat" broadcast on the evening of the invasion, Roosevelt said, "This nation will remain a neutral nation,

Isolationism

During the 1920s and 1930s, the majority of Americans believed that what went on outside the United States was not their business. They did not approve of dictatorial regimes, but they did not want the United States to get involved in world affairs. The casualties suffered by America in World War I only confirmed this view.

In order to ensure America's isolationism, Congress passed the 1935 and 1937 Neutrality Acts, which not only prevented American troops from going off to fight (except in self-defense) but prohibited the export of armaments to other countries at war. Roosevelt was not an isolationist himself—he had been a supporter of the League of Nations during President Wilson's administration—but he did not want to antagonize Congress while he was trying to get New Deal laws passed. He reluctantly accepted America's strict approach to neutrality.

but I cannot ask that every American remain neutral in thought as well. Even a neutral cannot be asked to close his mind or his conscience."

The French and British, who were now at war with Germany, desperately needed American arms and ammunition. Roosevelt at last began to gain supporters in Congress who believed that the

▲ *A grim-faced Roosevelt addresses a special session of Congress on September 26, 1939.*

neutrality laws were too strict, and toward the end of 1939 the prohibition against selling arms was lifted.

The success of Germany's *Blitzkrieg*, or "lightning war," against Western Europe in the spring of 1940 came as a wake-up call to America. Congress now began to take the threat of war seriously: it approved a massive buildup of the armed forces and a major weapons expansion program. This provided the catalyst for a drop in unemployment during this period —from 10 million in 1938 to half that number in 1941. Congress also took the unprecedented step of approving the nation's first peacetime draft.

A Third Term?

During 1940 FDR faced the difficult decision of whether or not to run for a third term as president—something no one had ever done before. The German conquest of France in June 1940 convinced him he should run again, and despite some opposition from his own party he won the Democratic nomination. Meanwhile, Britain, fighting Germany alone, was in a desperate position. The new British prime minister, Winston Churchill, needed extra ships to help defend Britain's sea routes from attack by German submarines. Bypassing Congress, Roosevelt used his presidential authority to send Britain 50 old destroyers in exchange for the use of British naval and air bases. This was an important step away from neutrality.

Roosevelt's Republican opponent during the 1940 election was Wendell Wilkie, who argued that it was dangerous to let any one person serve a third term and that Roosevelt was going to lead the country into war. Roosevelt denied these charges, but there can be little doubt that he had adopted policies that made war likely. Roosevelt comfortably won the election by 27 million to 22 million votes.

The Lend-Lease Act

Once reelected, Roosevelt felt confident enough to press forward and send arms to Britain. Roosevelt called America "the great arsenal of democracy," but the problem was that a nearly bankrupt Britain could not afford U.S. arms. Roosevelt proposed an imaginative solution: if Britain or any other nation could not afford to pay for arms, then they would be lent or leased to that country until the end of the war. The Lend-Lease Act was presented to Congress, and after much bitter opposition from isolationists, it was passed in March 1941. This greatly increased the flow of vital war supplies to Britain—and to the Soviet Union after Hitler's invasion in June 1941.

Roosevelt met Winston Churchill for the first time in August 1941, when the British prime minister traveled across the Atlantic in the battleship HMS *Prince of Wales*. The two leaders held secret talks that led to the Atlantic Charter, the agreement that proclaimed national self-determination and several freedoms

▶ *Roosevelt's opponent in 1940 was Wendell Wilkie, shown here during a campaign parade.*

Job No   :CG 02-008   Trim Size   :W 187 mm X H 229 mm
Job Title:20th Century History Maker Roosevelt   Paper Stock :Matt Art
Client   :The Watt Group   Screen   :#150

including freedom from want and freedom from fear. The two men—who had similar naval backgrounds—got along well together and would meet several times over the next few years.

The Drift Toward War

Roosevelt suffered a personal blow in September, when his mother Sara died at the age of 85, but given the seriousness of the international situation, the President had little time to grieve. German submarines had attacked American shipping in the Atlantic, and U.S. Navy destroyers began to escort Allied shipping part of the way across the Atlantic. By early December 1941, the United States and Germany were drifting toward war. Roosevelt was criticized for allowing this slide into conflict, but he felt it was essential that the United States act as a bulwark against totalitarian regimes. "If Great Britain goes down," he warned the American people, "the Axis powers will control the continents of Europe, Asia, Africa, Australasia, and the high seas— and they will be in a position to bring

enormous military and naval resources against this hemisphere."

But it was events in the Pacific region that most worried Roosevelt. After the fall of France in 1940, the Japanese had taken over French colonial possessions in Indochina and were threatening the oil fields in the Dutch East Indies. Hoping to contain Japanese expansion in the Pacific, the United States declared a trade embargo on Japan, which deprived it of many vital goods. The Japanese government reacted angrily to this decision and prepared to strike a knockout blow against the United States and Britain.

◀ *Roosevelt and Churchill on board HMS* Prince of Wales *after the signing of the Atlantic Charter on August 14, 1941.*

The Commander-in-Chief

The Japanese attack on the U.S. naval base at Pearl Harbor, on December 7, 1941, caught the Americans completely by surprise.

The U.S. Pacific Fleet suffered a grievous blow. During the attack, five battleships were sunk and three others badly damaged, and 2,335 U.S. servicemen were killed. The destruction of Pearl Harbor was the signal for an all-out Japanese offensive against American, British, and Dutch possessions in the Pacific and Southeast Asia.

On December 8, a grave and angry President Roosevelt addressed both houses of Congress and told them that the 7th would be a day that would "live in infamy." Congress then declared war on Japan. A few days later, Germany joined its Japanese Axis partner and declared war on the United States. The war was now a truly global conflict.

According to the terms of the U.S. Constitution, the President is also the Commander-in-Chief of all the armed forces, and Roosevelt assumed this

▶ *The battleship USS* West Virginia *burns after the Japanese attack on Pearl Harbor, December 7, 1941.*

Job No   : CG 02-008   Trim Size   : W 187 mm X H 229 mm
Job Title: 20th Century History Maker Roosevelt   Paper Stock   : Matt Art
Client   : The Watt Group   Screen   : #150   Colour 5

position with his customary relish for action. In fact, he preferred to be known by his military title rather than the more usual "Mr. President." Roosevelt dominated the American war effort. He assembled a talented circle of military advisers led by General George C. Marshall, his chief of staff. FDR felt free to impose his own ideas on matters such as overall strategy and the selection of key field commanders, but once a decision had been made, the military side of things was left to the man on the ground.

Roosevelt's first objective was to defeat the enemy, but he also wanted to end the conditions that had led to the outbreak of war in the first place—he hoped that the post-war world would be a more peaceful one. And he also realized that to defeat the enemy he would need to forge close relations with his allies, even though they might have very different war aims. As the United States was the world's greatest economic power, it became the leader in the war against Germany and Japan—the only country to play a leading role in the defeat of both these nations.

◀ *A patriotic wartime image of Roosevelt from 1942.*

The Big Three

FDR was always very aware that he must keep the Allied coalition together to defeat Germany and Japan. Sometimes this meant making difficult decisions, such as having to accept the demands of the Soviet leader Joseph Stalin. Roosevelt, Churchill, and Stalin—the "Big Three"—met for the first time in the Iranian capital of Teheran in November 1943. There they agreed to launch the long-awaited "second front" —the Anglo-American invasion of Europe, which had been demanded by Stalin in order to take pressure off his forces fighting the Germans in Russia.

After Teheran, Roosevelt was optimistic that the Allied leaders could bring about a lasting peace once the war was over. In retrospect, it would seem that he was unduly optimistic, not fully realizing the determination of the Soviet leader to turn Eastern Europe into a buffer zone to prevent any subsequent attack on the Soviet Union.

On January 1, 1942, the Allied countries—primarily the United States, Britain, the Soviet Union, and China—accepted the "Declaration of the United Nations." They agreed to keep fighting until final victory and to build a peacekeeping organization—which eventually became the United Nations—once victory was won.

But in the first half of 1942, victory seemed a very distant prospect. The Japanese had overrun the Philippines, Malaya, Burma, the Dutch East Indies, and many Pacific islands, repeatedly humiliating the Allies on the battlefield. The German army was pushing deep into the Soviet Union and inflicting defeats on the British in North Africa, while German U-boats were sinking a vast tonnage of Allied shipping, especially along the U.S. eastern coast.

For most Americans, the Japanese seemed the main threat, but Roosevelt and General Marshall decided on a "Germany First" policy. This meant that

the United States devoted its main effort to the war in Europe, with the Pacific front taking second place—although America's resources were large enough to ensure that its forces in the Pacific were not starved of men and armaments.

The Allied counterattack began when the British defeated the Axis forces at El Alamein in October 1942, which was followed by the U.S.-led invasion of North Africa in November. Although the Americans suffered some early losses, the Allies ejected the Axis forces from North Africa in May 1943. This was the prelude to the Allied invasion of Sicily and Italy, and the surrender of Italy to the Allies in September 1943.

While the fighting in North Africa was still going on, Roosevelt flew over to Morocco and discussed the conduct of the war with Churchill at the Casablanca Conference of January 1943. They agreed that while an invasion of Western Europe was necessary to win the war, the Allies would, in the meantime, step up their bombing campaign against German cities. They also agreed that that they would accept only an "unconditional surrender" from Germany, which in effect meant the total destruction of the Nazi system.

For the invasion of Europe, Roosevelt decided to appoint General Dwight D. Eisenhower to lead the Allied forces. This proved an exceptionally wise choice:

◀ *U.S. soldiers wade ashore on the beaches of northern France on "D-Day," June 6, 1944.*

although Eisenhower was not an experienced battlefield commander, he was a very good manager of men, and he was able to get the best out of his difficult and argumentative subordinate commanders, notably the British general Bernard Montgomery and the American general George Patton.

The Allied invasion was a brilliant success: well over 100,000 men were landed on the northern coast of France on the first day of fighting, June 6, 1944. With the arrival of reinforcements—and after much heavy fighting—the Allies drove the Nazi armies back to Germany. Early in 1945 the Allied armies fought their way into Germany, and by the end of April Hitler had killed himself and all remaining resistance was overcome.

The Yalta Conference

Roosevelt attended one last major conference of the "Big Three" at Yalta in February 1945. The division of Germany between the major powers was agreed upon, and Roosevelt and

▶ The "Big Three" at Yalta, from left, Churchill, Roosevelt, and Stalin, in February 1945.

Churchill accepted Stalin's promises that there would be free elections in Eastern Europe, which turned out to be false. Roosevelt, in particular, has been accused of being too easy on Stalin, but as the Soviet Union was the major military force in Eastern Europe there was little he could do to prevent Stalin's domination of that area. Indeed, Stalin had made it clear that he would not accept interference in Eastern Europe. Poland was a major

sticking point. "For the Russian people," said Stalin, "Poland is not only a question of honor, but a question of security. Throughout history, Poland has been the corridor through which the enemy has passed into Russia." Reluctantly, Roosevelt and Churchill had to accept military reality and concede the loss of Eastern Europe and the Balkans to Stalin—or risk the outbreak of World War III.

The Birth of the U.N.

FDR was determined that the new United Nations, which emerged from the war, would not suffer the weaknesses of the pre-war League of Nations. He reasoned that the League suffered from the intervention of too many small states. So, in the blueprint for the United Nations, which was laid down at Dumbarton Oaks, Washington, D.C., in October 1944, it was decided that the main Allied powers—the United States, Soviet Union, Great Britain, China, and France—would have a deciding role in the running of the organization. Although this may not have been strictly fair, it did help the U.N. work better in practice. It was another important achievement, and it was one that owed much to Roosevelt's own personal involvement.

Mopping Up the Pacific

In the Pacific, the Americans painfully and resolutely forced the Japanese back to their home islands. The fighting was tough and vicious, much of it consisting of American assaults on small islands that were defended to the last man by the Japanese. At sea, the U.S. Navy defeated the Japanese in a series of battles culminating in Leyte Gulf in October 1944—the largest naval battle in history.

By the summer of 1945, the Japanese no longer had an effective fighting force, but fears that an invasion of Japan itself might still lead to massive Allied casualties, the Americans turned to their secret weapon—the atomic bomb. As early as 1939, leading Allied scientists had warned Roosevelt of the possibility of the existence of an atom bomb—and that the Germans were working on such a project. Although, as a non-scientist, Roosevelt was slow to understand the real nature of this devastating weapon, he did authorize scientists to work on the project, and by 1945 two bombs were ready for use. These were the bombs that were dropped on Hiroshima and Nagasaki —causing catastrophic damage to the cities and their inhabitants—after which the Japanese surrendered. World War II was over.

America's Post-War Profile

During the war Roosevelt tried to make sure that once the fighting had ended, the United States would play an important role in the world. He managed to persuade the majority of the American people that a return to isolation was no longer a viable option. It worked and he won the support of the bulk of the American population; according to a 1944 Gallup poll, some 73 percent of the people thought that the U.S. should "take an active part in world affairs after the war." Roosevelt made this point in his 1945 inaugural address, when he said,

"We have learned that we cannot live alone, at peace; that our own well-being is dependent on the well-being of other nations far away."

FDR and the Home Front

World War II, ironically, accomplished what the New Deal was never able to manage: it rescued the American economy from the Great Depression.

◀ *The war years saw a huge increase in the output from U.S. factories. This photo shows Dauntless dive bombers on an assembly line.*

Industry was given a kick-start by the demand for war goods that followed the outbreak of war in Europe in 1939, although it was the military response to the Japanese attack on Pearl Harbor that transformed the economy and the nation.

Roosevelt's main role on the home front was to mobilize the population and industry to get behind the war effort. Congress gave the President great powers to organize the nation. As in the New Deal years, special agencies were set up to direct increased production. The War Production Board and the Reconstruction Corporation looked after goods and services, while the War Manpower Commission was responsible for sending the industrial workforce where it was most needed. One of the most important —and completely secret—decisions Roosevelt made during these years was to give the go-ahead to the Manhattan Project, which led to the construction of the atom bomb (see p. 91).

Roosevelt was criticized for introducing too many boards and agencies whose responsibilities overlapped, so that they often got in each other's way. There was some truth to this charge, and it was certainly true that Roosevelt liked to

Job No : CG 02-008
Job Title: 20th Century History Maker Roosevelt
Client   : The War C...

Trim Size   : W 187 mm X H 229 mm
Paper Stock

have competition between his subordinates and their organizations. In October 1942, in an attempt to impose order on the system, Roosevelt set up the Office of Economic Stabilization under the control of James F. Byrnes, whose job was to control wages, prices, and profits.

Whatever the failings of the federal government's organization of the war effort, it was more than offset by the amazing increase in military strength and industrial output. In 1939 the U.S. Army had only 186,000 men under arms, and ranked 19th as a world military power. By 1943 more than 12 million men and women were under arms, and America surpassed Germany and even the Soviet Union as the most powerful military force in the world.

The chief consequence of this economic revival was a dramatic fall in unemployment and a rise in general prosperity. From the "Roosevelt Recession" of 1937–1938, when unemployment figures had reached around 10 million, they fell back to 5.6 million in 1941 and then to just 670,000 in 1944—a mere 1.2 percent of the working population. The demand for workers drove up wages, and in some

World War II Industrial Output

The figures for U.S. industrial output were staggering. Armament factories produced 300,000 aircraft and 90,000 armored fighting vehicles, while shipyards launched more than 100,000 vessels, which included 88,000 landing craft, 350 destroyers, 200 submarines, and nearly 150 aircraft carriers. By 1944 the United States was producing some 60 percent of the Allies' total combat munitions. Indeed, so great was American war output that by 1944 factories were ordered to scale down production because there were not enough soldiers, sailors, and airmen to use the equipment.

areas of the United States formerly poor workers began to experience a degree of real prosperity.

Roosevelt did his utmost to encourage people working in war industries to feel a part of the overall struggle against the Axis powers. He wrote, "I know that all civilian war workers will be glad to say many years hence to their grandchildren: 'Yes, I, too, was in service in the great war. I was on duty in an airplane factory, and I helped make hundreds of fighting planes.'"

▶ *"We Can Do It!" This U.S. World War II poster features a woman munitions worker.*

▼ *Japanese-Americans board a train on their way to a detention camp in 1942.*

Japanese-Americans

The racial group that suffered most during the war were the Japanese-Americans, most of whom lived on America's west coast. After Pearl Harbor they were suspected of having Japanese sympathies and it was thought that they might act as secret agents for Japan. Pressure from the Army, local politicians, and a hysterical media led Roosevelt to sign the order for their forcible detention. Over 110,000 Japanese-Americans were sent to detention camps and most remained there, in poor conditions, until 1944.

Apart from the drop in unemployment, the single most striking feature of America's new war economy was the vast migration of people within the country. Besides the 12 million people who were drawn into the armed services, a further 16 million civilians traveled across the United States to work in the new war-related industries.

Women and War Work

Encouraged by the government, around six million women entered the workplace for the first time—many of them working in factories. Nicknamed the "Jane who makes the planes" or "Rosie the riveter,"

these blue-collar female workers were a new feature in American industrial life. For the women, regular well-paid employment gave many of them a degree of economic power and social freedom never enjoyed before.

The United States's large African-American population also experienced radical change during the war. New work opportunities led to higher standards of living, but at the price of increased racial tension as African-Americans left the rural South and went to the industrial Northeast, the Midwest, and California. The prejudice directed at African-Americans led to several race riots, the most violent on the streets of Detroit when 29 people were killed.

In order to provide some legal protection for African-Americans in the workplace, Roosevelt set up the Fair Employment Practices Committee in 1941, and this led to the Fair Employment Practices Act. The act banned discrimination in government departments and defense industries, but while it may have been the first example of civil-rights legislation, it was only of limited use in helping African-Americans get a better deal in the workplace.

Roosevelt's Health Fails

As the 1944 presidential elections neared, it was clear that Roosevelt's health was failing. He was exhausted from spending 12 years in office and suffered from heart problems. But Roosevelt felt he could not decline to run, saying: "If the people command me to continue in this office and in this war, I have as little right to withdraw as the soldier has to leave his post in the line." Fearing that he might not survive his next term, FDR's advisors persuaded him to accept the tough-minded Harry S. Truman as his vice president, in the knowledge that Truman would probably have to take over the presidency at some point.

The Republican opponent, Governor Thomas E. Dewey of New York, attacked the president on health grounds and for allowing "the communists to seize control of the New Deal." Roosevelt dealt with these accusations easily, ridiculing Dewey and the Republicans; he also spent several hours traveling the streets of New York in an open-topped car to show an appreciative crowd how well he was feeling.

FDR knew that, as the war was coming to an end, it was essential that the peace must work, not only on the international stage but for ordinary Americans— especially the many millions who would be returning from the armed forces. He announced that proper health care, education, jobs, and decent housing were to be a right for all in America, "where all persons regardless of race, and color, or creed or place of birth, can live in peace and honor and human dignity." Once again the people listened to Roosevelt, and he comfortably beat his presidential opponent for the fourth time.

Shortly after the election, FDR spent time recuperating at Warm Springs, and on January 20, 1945, he returned to Washington for his fourth inauguration, accompanied by his 13 grandchildren. He then traveled to the Soviet Union to attend the grueling Yalta Conference. On his return in March, he reported back to Congress, speaking for the first time to the assembled senators and congressmen from a wheelchair. All those present could see the strain that Roosevelt was under—and that he was not well.

▶ *An ill-looking Roosevelt with his vice-president elect, Harry S. Truman, in 1944.*

Job No   :CG 02-008
Job Title:20th Century History Maker Roosevelt

Trim Size   :W 187 mm X H 229 mm
Paper Stock   : Matt Art

Roosevelt returned to Warm Springs, having told those around him that with some rest he would "be in trim again." A few days later he agreed to sit to have his portrait painted. On April 12, while the artist worked, Roosevelt suddenly complained of having a "terrific headache" and then slumped forward in his chair unconscious. He had suffered a massive brain hemorrhage, and within two hours he was pronounced dead.

The nation was stunned by Roosevelt's death. As his body was taken by train from Warm Springs to Washington, thousands of mourners lined the route to pay their last respects, many openly weeping for their lost president. On April 14, Roosevelt's body, accompanied by Eleanor and the family, was taken from Washington to its last resting place at his old house of Springfield in Hyde Park, where he was buried in the rose garden.

▶ *An honor guard lines the route as Roosevelt's coffin travels through Washington, D.C., in 1945.*

The Roosevelt Legacy

The influence Franklin D. Roosevelt had on the life of the nation was arguably greater than that of any other president in the history of the United States.

This was partly because he had won four elections and served as president for 12 years. But it was also a result of his energetic and farsighted tackling of two of the greatest problems of the first half of the 20th century: the Great Depression and World War II.

Roosevelt greatly increased the role of federal government in the lives of the American people, a role that has continued and even increased in the present day. He also made the post of president far more important than it had been before. Although, like all leaders, FDR was forced to react to events, he also tried to shape them, and he became the nation's chief policy-maker, both in domestic and foreign affairs. He went beyond the traditional role of the president of looking after the interests of

the wealthy to protect the interests of the poor and weak. FDR was, to a certain extent, prepared to use the government as an instrument for social justice.

Despite the limitations of the New Deal, Roosevelt laid down the foundations for the "semi-welfare state" we see in America today. Some critics argue that as a result of these changes the federal government has become too powerful and that it strangles individual initiative. Whatever the rights and wrongs of this debate, there can be little doubt that they are a consequence of Roosevelt's New Deal policies.

FDR can also be called the first modern president. Instead of allowing himself to

▶ *Roosevelt was mourned around the world. Here, Eleanor and Britain's King George VI unveil a statue in FDR's honor in Grosvenor Square, London, in 1948.*

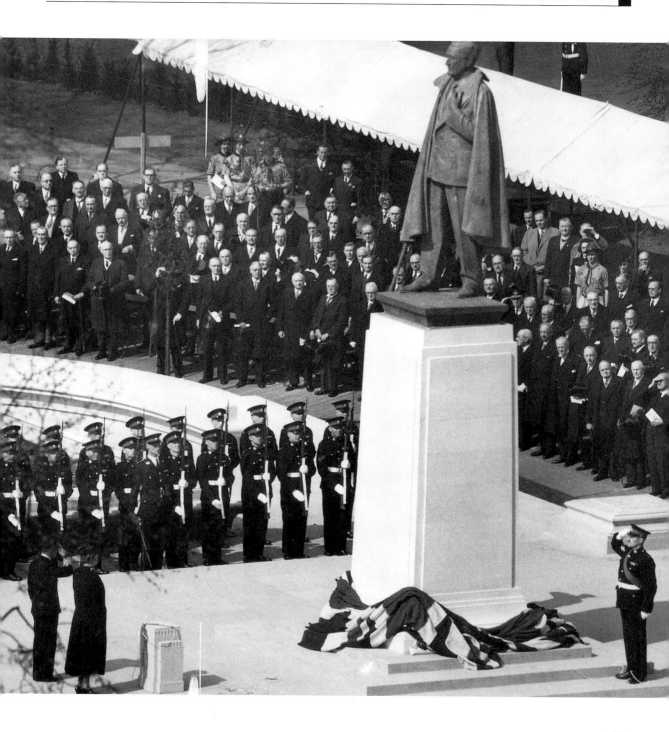

be confined to the White House and the political world of Washington, D.C., he embraced the media—newspapers, newsreels, and especially the radio—to reach out and communicate directly with the people. The people liked what they saw and heard, and consistently voted in favor of Roosevelt and against his less charismatic and non-media-friendly opponents. All presidential candidates since Roosevelt have had to be able to use the media to have any chance of electoral success.

The other main area of Roosevelt's legacy, still crucial today, is in leading the U.S. away from its traditional position of isolationism toward to one of intervention—to involve the country in the affairs of the wider world. Through his "fireside chats," FDR helped educate the American people to look beyond the national horizon.

Roosevelt drew upon the frustrations he had experienced in the years immediately after the end of World War I, to ensure that the new international organizations would be powerful enough to have an impact on the world after 1945. The tragedy for Roosevelt was that he did not live to see the success of agencies such as the United Nations and the International Monetary Fund, which owed so much to his personal vision.

Roosevelt was also inspirational in his own reaction to disability. Not only did he deal with the terrible setback of suffering polio with courage and cheerfulness, he made great efforts to help fellow sufferers. At Warm Springs he encouraged scientists and doctors to find a cure for polio, and he helped set up the "March of Dimes" organization, where people across the country contributed as little or as much as they could afford to help find a cure. In fact, a vaccine was developed in 1954— nine years after FDR's death—which was able to protect the population from polio. Today the disease is virtually unknown in the West. The example he set to others— that they too could triumph over disability, of whatever kind—is one that remains with us today.

The historian Arthur Schlesinger, Jr. aptly summed up Roosevelt's life: "He lifted the U.S. out of economic despair and revolutionized the American way of life. Then he helped make the world safe for democracy."

▶ *An informal portrait of FDR and his dog, Fala, taken at a 1941 press conference.*

Glossary

Allies In World War I, those countries who fought against Germany, Austria-Hungary, and Turkey. In World War II, those countries who fought against Germany, Italy, and Japan—including Great Britain, France, the Soviet Union, and the United States.

Axis In World War II, the alliance of Germany, Italy, and Japan that fought the Allies.

Blitzkrieg A German word meaning "lightning war," used to describe the fast-moving tactics developed by Germany during World War II.

capitalism The economic system in which the production of goods and services depends on the investment of money (capital) in exchange for the making of a financial profit.

communism An extreme political theory and system of government in which everything is owned by the state and where economic activity is directed by the state for the benefit of all.

Congress The law-making (legislative) part of the American government that comprises two "houses": the House of Representatives and the Senate. A Congressman/woman is a member of the House of Representatives; he or she is elected every two years. Congress is the second branch of the federal government, alongside the presidency (first) and the Supreme Court (third).

Constitution The list of rules by which the United States is governed.

Convention The great public meeting where the candidate of the Democratic or Republican Party is chosen to run in the presidential election.

Democratic Party One of the two main American political parties—opposed by the Republican Party.

depositor An individual who puts (deposits) his or her money into a bank.

draft The American system of conscription, where young men (and sometimes women) are required to serve in the armed forces.

federal government The national government of the United States, based in Washington, D.C., comprising the presidency, Congress, and the Supreme Court.

first lady The wife of the President.

Great Depression The period in the early 1930s when a vast economic slump affected industrial nations around the world, leading to widespread unemployment and poverty.

hydroelectricity A means of producing electricity using water power.

inauguration The ceremony in which the winner of the presidential election is sworn in as president of the United States.

League of Nations An international organization set up after World War I to resolve disputes between countries in a peaceful manner.

left-wing To believe in greater involvement of the state in the economic life of the nation and in increased taxation of the better-off to support the less well-off. The opposite of right-wing.

migration The movement of large numbers of people within a country.

presidential election Held every four years in November to decide who is to be the next U.S. President. Roosevelt won the 1932, 1936, 1940, and 1944 elections.

Republican Party One of the main political parties in the United States—opposed by the Democratic Party.

right-wing To discourage the state's involvement in the economic life of the nation; to encourage people to look after themselves.

running mate The person nominated as vice president during the presidential elections.

senator A member of the Senate, one of the two parts of Congress.

socialism Not as extreme as communism but a left-wing political theory that encourages the state's direction of people's lives.

state One of the 48 states that made up the United States of America in Roosevelt's time.

Supreme Court The third (judicial) branch of the federal government. One of the main tasks of the Supreme Court is to ensure that laws passed do not break the rules of the Constitution.

United Nations Formed in 1945 as an organization of all the world's countries (states) to prevent war and encourage international cooperation.

Time Line

January 30, 1882 Franklin Delano Roosevelt born at Hyde Park

September 1896 Enters Groton School, Massachusetts

1900 Accepted at Harvard University

1904 Attends Columbia Law School

March 17, 1905 Marries distant cousin Eleanor Roosevelt

June 1907 Joins Wall Street law firm

November 1910 Elected as a Democrat to the New York State Senate

1912 Re-elected to the Senate; Woodrow Wilson elected President

March 1913 Appointed Assistant Secretary of the Navy

1914 Outbreak of World War I

April 1917 The United States enters World War I on the Allied side

November 1918 Allied victory in World War I

July 1920 Democrats nominate James Cox for president with Roosevelt as vice president;

November Republicans under Warren G. Harding defeat Democrats

August 1921 Contracts crippling disease of poliomyelitis (polio)

1927 Establishes Warm Springs spa in Georgia as a treatment center for people suffering from polio

November 1928 Elected as governor of New York; Herbert Hoover elected President

October 1929 Wall Street Crash: the stock market collapses

August 1931 Establishment of New York State's Temporary Emergency Relief Administration

November 1932 Defeats Hoover and is elected President of the United States

March 4, 1933 Inauguration as President; **May 12** Creation of Federal Emergency Relief Administration (FERA) and Agricultural Adjustment Administration (AAA); **May 18** Creation of Tennessee Valley Authority (TVA); **June 16** Creation of National Recovery Administration (NRA) and Public Works Administration (PWA)

April 1935 Creation of Works Progress Administration (WPA); **May** Supreme Court invalidates the NRA and AAA; **July** Wagner Act creates the National Labor Relations Board (NLRB); **August** Passing of the Social Security Act; **September 8** Assassination of Huey Long

November 1936 Defeats Republican Alfred Landon in the presidential election, to begin second term; **December 29** Beginning of sitdown strike at the General Motors (GM) factory

February 1937 The Judiciary Reorganization ("Court-packing") Bill is submitted to Congress, and is subsequently rejected; **May** Passing of Neutrality Act; **September** Beginning of "Roosevelt Recession"

Further Reading

September 1939 German invasion of Poland leads to outbreak of World War II
June 1940 German victory in Western Europe; surrender of France; **September** United States gives Britain 50 destroyers in exchange for naval bases; **November** Defeats Wendell Wilkie in Presidential elections; beginning of third term
March 1941 Passing of Lend-Lease Act;
August 15 Signing of the Atlantic Charter;
December 7 Japanese attack on Pearl Harbor; Congress declares war on Japan
1942 Creation of War Labor Board; **February** Beginning of internment of Japanese-Americans;
November Allied forces land in North Africa
January 1943 Casablanca Conference (between FDR and Churchill); **November** Tehran Conference (between FDR, Churchill, and Stalin)
July 1944 Bretton Woods Conference lays down foundation of the World Bank and International Monetary Fund (IMF); **August–October** Dumbarton Oaks Conference establishes United Nations; **November** Defeats Republican Thomas E. Dewey in presidential elections
February 1945 Yalta Conference (between FDR, Churchill, and Stalin); **April 12** Death of Roosevelt; succeeded by Harry S. Truman;
September 2 Japanese surrender; end of World War II

Burgan, Michael. *Franklin D. Roosevelt*. New York: Compass Point Books, 2002.

Freedman, Russell. *Franklin Delano Roosevelt*. New York: Clarion Books, 1990.

Green, Robert. *Franklin Delano Roosevelt*. Chicago, IL: Ferguson Publishing Co., 2001.

Israel, Fred L., ed. *Franklin Delano Roosevelt*. New York: Chelsea House Publications, 1985.

Schuman, Michael A. *Franklin D. Roosevelt: The Four Term President*. Springfield, NJ: Enslow Publishers, 1996.

Taylor, David. *Franklin D. Roosevelt*. London: Heinemann, 2001.

Websites

Encyclopedia Americana: **www.gi.grolier.com**
Franklin D. Roosevelt Library & Museum: **www.fdrlibrary.marist.edu**
Franklin D. Roosevelt (biography): www. **spartacus.schoolnet.co.uk**
The Franklin and Eleanor Roosevelt Institute: **www.feri.org**

Index

Page numbers in italics are pictures or maps.